It's a Good Thing There Are
Bats

by Joanne Mattern

Content Consultant

Elizabeth Case DeSantis, M.A. Elementary Education
Julia A. Stark Elementary School, Stamford, Connecticut

Reading Consultant

Jeanne Clidas, Ph.D.
Reading Specialist

Children's Press®
An Imprint of Scholastic Inc.
New York Toronto London Auckland Sydney
Mexico City New Delhi Hong Kong
Danbury, Connecticut

Library of Congress Cataloging-in-Publication Data
Mattern, Joanne, 1963- author.
It's a good thing there are bats/by Joanne Mattern.
    pages cm. — (Rookie read-about science)
Summary: "Introduces the reader to bats and explains the roles they play in the
environment."— Provided by publisher.
Audience: Ages 3-6.
ISBN 978-0-531-22362-8 (library binding: alk. paper) — ISBN 978-0-531-22834-0 (pbk.: alk. paper)
    1. Bats—Juvenile literature. I. Title. II. Title: It is a good thing there are bats. III. Series:
Rookie read-about science.

QL737.C5M382 2015
    599.4—dc23   2014015494

Produced by Spooky Cheetah Press
Design by Keith Plechaty

© 2015 by Scholastic Inc.

Printed in China 62

SCHOLASTIC, CHILDREN'S PRESS, ROOKIE READ-ABOUT®, and associated logos
are trademarks and/or registered trademarks of Scholastic Inc.

4 5 6 7 8 9 10 R 24 23 22 21 20 19 18 17

Photographs ©: Alamy Images: 29 (Michael Lynch), 8 (PetStockBoys); Getty Images: 4 (Merlin
Tuttle), 27 bottom, 31 center bottom (Michael Durham), 28 top (Peter Charlesworth/LightRocket),
20 (WIN-Initiative); iStockphoto/photovideostock: cover background; Science Source: 15
(B.G. Thomson), 3 top left, 7, 12, 23, 27 top left, 31 center top, 31 bottom (Dr. Merlin D. Tuttle/
Bat Conservation International), 19 (Tony Camacho); Shutterstock, Inc./anshu18: 3 top right;
Superstock, Inc.: 30 top right (Don White), cover, 11, 16, 24, 27 top right, 28 bottom, 31 top (Minden
Pictures), 28 center (NHPA); Thinkstock: 3 bottom (Alexei Zaycev), 30 bottom (erniedecker), 30
top left (HappyToBeHomeless).

Table of Contents

It's a Good Thing...

Some people are scared of bats. They think that a bat might bite them. But it is a good thing there are bats!

This is a spotted bat.

A leaf-nosed bat snatches an insect right out of the air.

Bats do not hurt people. They help people in many ways. Some bats eat insects, such as mosquitoes. A little brown bat can eat up to 1,000 mosquitoes in just one hour!

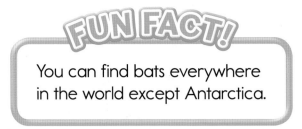

FUN FACT!

You can find bats everywhere in the world except Antarctica.

Some bats eat fruit. As they fly, the bats spread the seeds of the fruit so more can grow.

Some bats drink nectar from plants. As they fly from plant to plant, the bats spread pollen. That creates new plants, too.

This flying fox bat is eating a piece of fruit.

All About Bats

A bat is a **mammal**. A mammal's body is covered with fur or hair. Mammals are warm-blooded. They give birth to live young and feed them milk from their bodies.

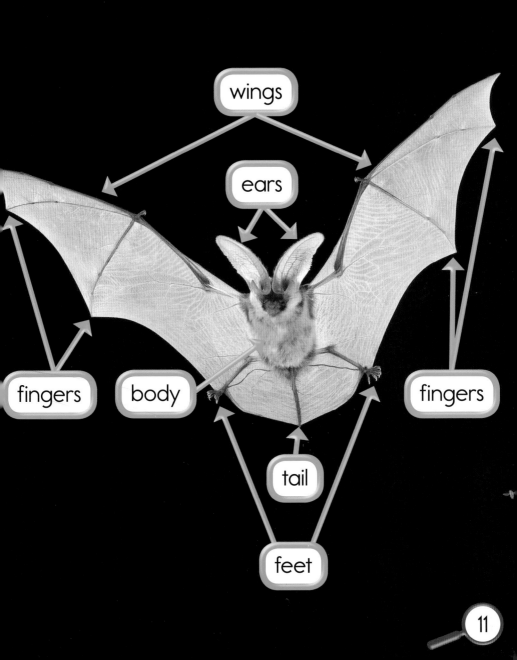

wings

ears

fingers

body

fingers

tail

feet

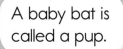

A baby bat is called a pup.

Mother bats give birth to one or two babies at a time. Baby bats stay close to their mother until they are bigger.

FUN FACT!

Bats are the only mammals that can fly.

Most bats are **nocturnal**. They sleep during the day and hunt at night.

Some bats find their **prey** by making squeaky sounds. These sounds create echoes that tell the bat where its prey is. This is called **echolocation**.

This bat's big ears help it locate prey.

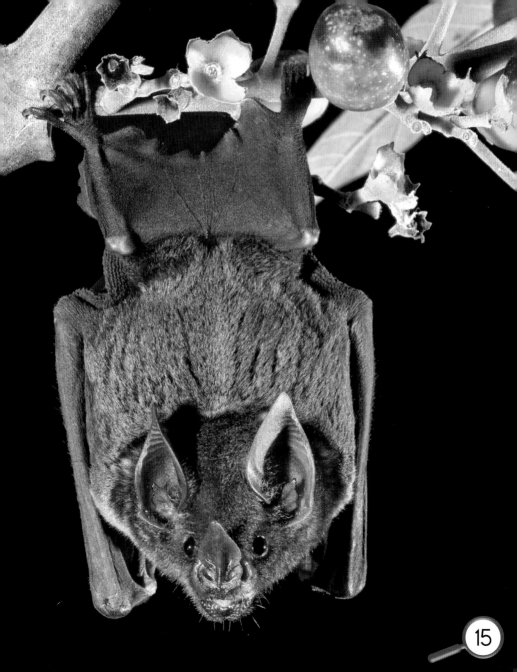

Mega Bats

Mega bats live in hot, wet places in Australia, Asia, and Africa. There are more than 180 different kinds of mega bats.

This is a great fruit-eating bat.

Bats hang upside down when they sleep.

Mega bats eat fruit. They do not use echolocation to find food.

FUN FACT!

Some bats live for more than 20 years.

Mega bats' ears are small. They do not hear as well as other bats do. A mega bat has large eyes and a long nose. It can see and smell very well.

Micro Bats

Micro bats are small bats. The smallest micro bat is the bumblebee bat. It weighs about as much as a dime.

Another name for the bumblebee bat is Kitti's hog-nosed bat.

ears

Micro bats fly around at night eating insects. They have big ears. Micro bats use echolocation to find their prey in the dark.

This is a White-throated Round-eared bat eating an insect.

Both mega and micro bats are helpful to people. That's why it's a good thing there are bats!

Bats Are Good For...

...pollinating flowers.

...spreading fruit seeds.

...eating insects.

The largest mega bat is the **Malayan flying fox.** This bat weighs about 5 pounds (2 kilograms). Its wingspan is 6 feet (2 meters).

Bats have been around for a long time! Scientists have found **bat fossils** from 55 million years ago.

Some bats, like the **greater bulldog bat**, go fishing for their dinner.

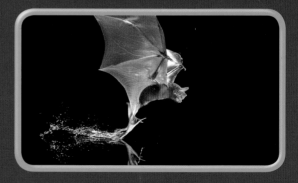

Feature Fun

Vampire bats drink animal blood. A spot on the bat's nose can sense heat. That helps the bat find the best feeding place on an animal's body. Unlike a lot of other types of bats, vampire bats can walk, run, and jump.

Q. What animals make the best baseball players?

A. Bats!

Q. What circus performers can see in the dark?

A. Acro-bats!

Creature Feature Fun

Which habitat is right for bats?

A

B

Answer: B. Bats do not live on the frozen continent of Antarctica.

Give Bats a Hand

Bats need safe places to live. You can help by placing a bat house in your yard. You can find kits for these houses in stores or find instructions on the Internet on how to build one. Ask an adult to help you—and you will be helping bats keep your neighborhood mosquito-free!

Glossary

echolocation (e-koe-loe-KAY-shun): using high-pitched sounds that bounce off objects and travel back to show where prey is

mammal (MAM-uhl): warm-blooded animal that gives birth to live young and produces milk to feed them

nocturnal (nok-TUR-nuhl): active at night

prey (PRAY): animal that is hunted by another animal for food

Index

Facts for Now

Visit this Scholastic Web site for more information on bats:
www.factsfornow.scholastic.com
Enter the keyword **Bats**

About the Author

Joanne Mattern is the author of many books for children. Animals are her favorite subject to write about! She lives in New York State with her husband, four children, and numerous pets, and often sees little brown bats in her yard on summer nights.